BEFORE THE

DA VINCI

BEFORE THE
DA VINCI

An Introduction to the Original
Encoded Secret Concerning
Jesus, Mary, and a Child

J. S. Tyson

EcceNova Editions
Victoria, BC

For copyright licenses, please contact: Access Copyright, 1 Yonge Street, Suite 1900, Toronto, ON M5E 1E5
www.accesscopyright.ca

Library and Archives Canada Cataloguing in Publication

Tyson, Janet, 1962-
Before the da Vinci code : an introduction to the original encoded secret concerning Jesus, Mary and a child / J.S. Tyson.

ISBN 0-9735341-7-6

1. Jesus Christ—Historicity. 2. Bible. N.T. John—Criticism, interpretation, etc. I. Title.

BS2615.52.T96 2005 232.9'08 C2005-902824-6

Cover: Greek Papyrus 457 (Jn 18:31-33). Reproduced by courtesy of the Director and Librarian, the John Rylands University Library of Manchester, UK.

CONTENTS

PREFACE

Before Leonardo da Vinci's code – fact *or* fiction – there was a mysterious and contentious gospel. Centuries in the future it would be known as the Gospel According to John, or the Fourth Gospel. It was eloquent and sophisticated, and was cherished by the growing Christian Church as a unique glorification of the deity they called "Jesus Christ."

That gospel, however, began its existence in quite a different context. It told a very dangerous tale – one that would be suppressed as soon as Paul (Saul of Tarsus) realized its significance. It was written for a very specific audience, and its message, politically provocative and religiously challenging, was purposefully encoded, using numerology, symbolism, allusion, and a clever play on words, so that those who were neither "true believers" nor supporters of Jesus' Movement, could not easily discover the location of the new kingdom and thus pose a threat to it. Readers and listeners were taken through the plot, step by step, tested along the way for their ability to "see" and willingness to "follow."

The promulgators of this particular gospel would be branded heretics, its subversive and rebellious nature curtailed. Having proven so popular initially, however, and having amassed such a following, this account of Jesus' life could not be quelled completely, so, in a case of "If you can't beat them join them," the Church embraced the heretic gospel and used its mystery and deep symbolism to their advantage.

On April 25, 2005, at Passover, my seven-year investigation into the Gospel According to John was published. The book, entitled *Jesus, King of Israel: Samaritan Blood and the Kingdom at Shiloh*, is 300+ pages of intense attention to detail. It is a voyage of discovery through a gospel that was hijacked and shrouded in secrecy by a Church that had a very different story to tell. It is a complex account, interpreting every minor detail, revealing every little clue… it is not for the faint of heart. It was necessary for me to present the material in a semi-academic fashion, in order for the critics to follow and assess my line of reasoning.

I soon became aware, however, that in order to reach those who would truly appreciate what *Jesus, King of Israel* has to say, but who may not relish wading through pages of explanations, references to obscure biblical passages, and translations of Greek and Hebrew words, I would have to present a more palatable 'synopsis' of the entire tome. This, I hope, is just such an offering.

When Dan Brown's *The Da Vinci Code* made headlines, it seemed an obvious tie-in with my own fact-based, biblical-based work. When I began my research, I was an undergraduate; when I finished, I was a post-graduate fellow, with a book. I had no idea, early on, that such a serendipitous timing would occur – with the 'Jesus, Mary & Child' phenomenon becoming so mainstream yet so contentious. How apt, I thought, for the *truth* about the original, controversial, encoded secret to resurface, just as the world is becoming fascinated with the subject… albeit through a work of fiction!

Of course, there have been other biblical scholars who have claimed that Jesus was married and had a child, but this is not the be-all and end-all of *my* work. The tale of *Jesus, King of Israel* is far more than just who he was married to and whether or not he had any offspring... it changes the way we view both Christianity and Messianic Judaism. So, with this in mind, I present the following concise *Introduction to the Original Encoded Secret Concerning Jesus, Mary, and a Child*, in the hopes that it will whet your appetite for more detail and greater insight.

This synopsis will take you through the key elements of the story *behind* Jesus' controversial relationship with Mary Magdalene, and will explain the significance of the mysterious child. Everything in this little book relates to research fully presented in *Jesus, King of Israel*, so please refer to that work for evidence and supporting material.

It is time for understanding.

J. S. Tyson

JESUS THE SAMARITAN

Have you ever read the book of 2 Esdras? I hadn't either, when I first started my research. In fact, I didn't read it until about half way along the seven-year journey through the gospel. I forget which clue brought me there, but suddenly, I found myself reading the story of Jesus… in the Apocrypha!

The narrator of 2 Esdras is a character called Salathiel, a.k.a. Ezra. He begins his mission, he tells us, after thirty years of traveling around the world, seeing how ungodly the nations have become. He is told by a sage that Israel has been entrusted to him, and that he will serve as their shepherd. There are signs and wonders, but many mock him and reject him. He is eventually "handed over to the many" after being judged, and is hung on a tree. There are references to "the third day," to the consecrated "twelve," and to a plethora of apparently Christian concepts… yet, how often do you hear this book mentioned?

Christian scholars are at a loss as to how to refer to 2 Esdras, so most don't. It is like an awkward family secret that can't quite be swept under the carpet, but no one wants to talk about it. In fact, 2 Esdras is probably the earliest and most authentic account of the Jesus of history that we have. Remarkably, it mirrors both the content and the literary style of the Gospel of John (e.g., it uses many parallel phrases and concepts, and employs an ambiguity, with respect to the voices of the two main characters, that reflects the literary ambiguity in the gospel) – so much so that it helped to confirm much of what I had discovered independently about the philosophy behind Jesus' mission. 2 Esdras (or at least a major part of it) and the Gospel of John were, I contend, written at around the same time, and probably by the very same author(s).

...Salathiel, then, whom we can take to be Jesus, returns home after thirty-odd years abroad. Does he go to India and sit with the gurus? Probably. Does he set foot on the green land of England, as the song suggests? Possibly. That isn't the point. The point is, he sees how the world beyond his homeland functions without the god of his forefathers. He doesn't like what he sees. His faith in his own religion, his idealism, and his convictions become heightened and he embarks on a mission to guide the scattered remnant of true believers (true Israelites) back to a place of honour (which they have apparently lost somewhere along the way). When the righteous return to worship God in the manner expected of them, so Jesus believes, the oppressors will be vanquished and the Messiah will come.

That's right. Jesus anticipated the coming of a Messiah, too! In the Gospel of John, he never once claims that role for himself. Others try to thrust it upon him, but he rejects it. The only time he accepts the concept is when he is in Samaria, talking to the woman by the well – but we shall get to that scene later.

This brings us to the question, "Where was Jesus' home?" The knee-jerk reaction is to say Bethlehem, or Nazareth... but that would be the Christian, post-Jesus influence (yes, I did say that). Jesus' home, we soon discover in the gospel, *is* Samaria. He is Samaritan by birth and it is the Samaritan ideal to which he aspires, and is for which he is driven to action. As such he is a northerner, born into one of the nine northern tribes that would become known as the "lost" or "missing" tribes. The gospel makes it so evident *which* tribe this is; it is the one clue that is hiding in plain sight… Jesus is *called* the "son of Joseph," that is, he is a son of the family of Joseph. The Samaritans called themselves (and still do) the "sons of Joseph" – Jesus, we learn through complex but cohesive clues, is of the Josephite tribe of Ephraim. Jesus, son of Joseph becomes, to Semitic hearers of the gospel, *Joshua ben Joseph.*

As we shall witness, Jesus accepts the role not as the Davidic Messiah, but as the Samaritan, priestly messiah. He claims to have come to return the sons of Joseph to their rightful place as the elect of God. As such, his duty is to restore Israel to its pre-Sinai state – an idealized (perhaps) state of unity and purity. Israel was *intended* to be a "priestly kingdom," that is, having a high-priest-king, such as we see in Melchizedech, one of Jesus' role models. Jesus must somehow, even if only symbolically (i.e., to act as a sign to the nations that the time has come for change, if not to act as a call to arms!), gather the "lost" believers together and guide them to the new house of God. In order to have a new house of God, the Temple establishment must be rejected, a new priesthood inaugurated, the Ark of the Covenant and the holy anointing oil restored, and, most importantly, a hereditary line ensured.

This is why Jesus, unlike so many of his contemporaries who attempted to seize control in the name of messianic fervor, who sought prestige, or glory, or simply wanted to fulfill their people's desire for emancipation, would leave his mark so indelibly on history, while others faded into the past with little more than a whisper about their efforts. His goal was so immense, his audacity so extreme, his perspective so unique, there was just no one to compare. Far from

7

being the poorly educated woodworker who 'loved little children' and went about telling everyone to "love each other," Jesus proves to be a relentless politician, a tenacious adversary, an astute tactician, and a focused, charismatic leader, who knows which buttons to press to get the most from people, be they opponents or supporters.

In the gospel, we also see Jesus assuming the role of his namesake, Joshua, the Josephite, who led the 'true believers' away from the southern, seemingly corrupt tribes of Judah, Simeon, and Benjamin (this in itself is an important element of the story, as much of what Jesus says and does in the gospel relates back to this ancient precedent; I expand on the Moses-Joshua scenarios in my book). Jesus' role as priest, especially high priest, however, is questioned, genealogically and ritually, by both the opposing authorities and even some of those who have been expecting such a 'messiah of the north', e.g., some of John the Baptist's followers, but Jesus maintains his position. After all, his vision is for a *new* priesthood, and it has to begin with *someone*!

Amazingly, there is yet *another* ancient tradition and body of literature that attests to a man who was deemed a northern messiah (a man very much like our Jesus) but which is relegated to obscurity by scholars who feel threatened by the implications. This body of literature and tradition is collectively known as the Messiah ben Joseph tradition. This messiah is a Josephite, he gathers hoards of supporters but many are killed by occupying forces; he is called "Son of Joseph," "Son of God," and "King of Israel"; he is slain and later revived; and after his death, many wonder if they had missed their opportunity to follow him. His death signals the eventual downfall of Jerusalem and the loss of the Temple.

For those who say there is no evidence for the historical Jesus outside of the New Testament… you couldn't be more wrong. It just depends on how open your mind is to alternatives, and what your perspective is. There is 2 Esdras. There is the Semitic tradition of the Messiah ben Joseph, and there are several, as yet unacknowledged references to the Jesus Movement (and even to Mary) in the writings of Flavius Josephus (*not* including the obvious references, which most scholars accept as later insertions). All of these accounts help build a vivid picture of who Jesus was and what he was attempting to do.

RIGHTS OF THE FIRSTBORN

The original Joshua, who took his anti-Egyptian, anti-Moses followers up to Samaria from Sinai, created a series of five sacred sites, the fifth of which was a place called Shiloh.

Now Shiloh is an interesting place. It is the only geographical location for which the Bible provides explicit and detailed directions. It is also very subtly embedded in a prophecy in, of all places, the Book of Genesis, that predicts the coming of the new King of Israel! What I suggest is that Jesus, whether inspired by his sage or not, adopts this prophecy (amongst other biblical precedents) as his own and devises a plan to oust the current religious rulers of Palestine... the Judeans, the Temple cultus.

At first, he thinks the takeover will be fairly simple. Once the people come to know the truth about how the royal and priestly throne was usurped from the family of Joseph by the leaders of Judea, how the southern tribes managed to lose the Ark of the Covenant *and* the sacred anointing oil; once they see how pandering to the iniquitous priesthood and their lackeys is tantamount to sacrificing their inheritance... surely, they will follow! But life just isn't that simple. Not even for Jesus. The Gospel of John describes how Jesus falters and is a poor judge of character, to begin with. He fails to recognize the spy within his own inner circle. He trusts the wrong people, and expects too much from those who just don't have his stamina or zeal.

He begins, however, by gathering his disciples. Though we learn, later, that there were twelve, only six are explicitly mentioned: Andrew, Judas, Peter, Philip, Nathanael, and Lazarus (yes, he is a disciple… we'll get to him, soon). We also learn that each has a tribal affiliation that is unique, and that each bears a "commission name." Commission names are one of the main keys to unraveling the gospel's clues. They represent a character's inner nature, or role, within a certain context. Some characters have only one such name, while others have several. It can seem confusing at first, but once you grasp the overall message of the gospel, you will see these as 'so obvious', you'll wonder why no one has noticed them before!

The disciples are a curious lot. There is Andrew, who is very Hellenistic in his thinking. Judas, who first makes his presence known as the unnamed initiate who follows Jesus on that first fateful night of induction after the infamous baptism (I say "infamous" because this scene is controversial in the Gospel of John, and points to more of a serious rivalry between John and Jesus). Of course, it will be Judas who turns out to be the infiltrator and the informer but Jesus doesn't have an inkling at this point. Peter, the Church's 'rock', turns out to be somewhat less than an asset. Philip, we discover, is actually one of Jesus' own sons, picked specifically for the job of becoming Jesus' right-hand-man and heir. Unfortunately, Philip proves that he just doesn't have his father's motivation or insight, and fails to live up to expectations. Nathaniel turns out to be far more significant than anyone had previously thought, becoming the representative for the 'remnant' of the faithful Jesus is so set on rescuing. As for Lazarus, well, he is arguably the most important character in the Gospel of John – perhaps even more so than Jesus. His story is so intertwined with Jesus' that, at times, it is hard to distinguish who is who in the narrative... and the author of the gospel makes this ambiguity *explicit* in at least two scenes. He does this for a very sound reason, which we will get to momentarily.

With these handful of disciples, then, Jesus sets out to seize the throne from the Judean usurpers. Of course, there is only a symbolic throne these days, with the nation under Roman occupation, but it is nonetheless vital. You see, if that obscure little Genesis prophecy is correct, the new ruler of the *united* Israel will build his kingdom at the sacred site of Shiloh. With that in place, the rest of the fate for the people of God is secured... the Messiah will come, freedom will follow, and the faithful will live happily ever after, in a purified and righteous priestly kingdom. So, the literal sense of overthrow doesn't really come into play; it is like a surreal, mystical game of chess, with the stakes purely emblematic. He who achieves checkmate, however, wins all.

So, what is the first public demonstration Jesus embarks upon with these disciples? The wedding at Cana. A strange choice, you might think. Well, what you need to remember from this point on, is that *everything* the gospel tells you is guiding you to Shiloh, step by step. It is up to you to decipher the clues and follow Jesus there. Every character, every action with its consequence, every so-called "miracle" has a purpose and serves as a signpost along the way. What happens in reality also has a symbolic counterpart, and vice versa. The wedding is the first such sign.

The wedding takes place on the third day, a commonly used reference to a sacred day of union between the divine and the faithful. We learn that the marriage, apart from being a symbolic allusion to the reunion of the tribes, is the actual union of Jesus' own daughter and the golden-boy, Nathanael. The water-into-wine event, though highly provocative, is not a miracle – in fact, there are no miracles in this gospel, just carefully orchestrated events that have precise meanings.

As the plot continues, Jesus decides it is time to let the people, en masse, into the picture. He demonstrates his intentions by making a public display at the Temple, turning over the tables and wielding a whip. Yes, many scholars have pointed to various biblical precedents for this scene, but what is important to note is that Jesus is not doing this to denounce the rite of sacrifice, or to reject the sale of sacrificial animals within the Temple precinct... he is making a very clear assault on the establishment itself. This is just one instance where a detailed analysis of the original language of the gospel (Koine Greek) becomes valuable, for we discover that Jesus' diatribe is focused on the inner sanctum of the Temple – the "*naos,*" the seat of the high priest, whom Jesus calls the "father of lies." This one act, so carefully staged, sends shockwaves through the priestly community – at this point they, too, know exactly what Jesus is here for.

There is a theme that runs through various books in the Bible, about the unlawful tenants being ousted, and the rightful heir... the firstborn... being reinstated. This is brought to bear on the cultus that has squandered the inheritance of the firstborn (i.e., they have seized what is rightfully Joseph's. Again, this is explained in detail in my other book). Jesus is angry, and he shows it. And don't be lulled into a false sense of 'divine wrath', here... this is real, human anger. Jesus is using a violent action to convey a powerful message – and it won't be the last time he utilizes a little 'pressure' this way.

From now on, Jesus has to watch his back.

He makes his strongest and most influential alliance, ironically, with the priest and Pharisee, Nicodemus. The entire dialogue between Nicodemus and Jesus is paralleled in that between Uriel and Ezra, in 2 Esdras. It is uncanny. Basically, what is being said is that in order to follow Jesus, one has to *put aside previously-held convictions* and trust him. The dialogue also teaches us, as the readers of the gospel, to put aside our own preconceptions (e.g., primarily of Christian interpretation, in our case) and to follow the clues the author has presented for us. Nicodemus' transformation anticipates our own.

The subsequent major focus in the gospel narrative is the meeting of Jesus and the woman at the well, back in Samaria. This is when Jesus makes his Samaritan affiliation crystal clear. He manages to convince this woman, and her family, that he is the one they have been waiting for – the priestly messiah from their own people. He explains how she has "had five husbands," but we, the careful detectives, soon learn that this refers to the five sacred places for the Samaritans… those five sacred places Joshua created after leaving Sinai. The woman becomes a *representative* of her people, another common literary tactic in the gospel that proves quite enlightening. The sixth "husband" who is "not a husband" (the riddle) is the mountain on which the Samaritans now worship, Mount Gerizim. Shiloh, the fifth and final resting place for the Ark of the Covenant is the last, rightful "husband."

When the woman realizes what Jesus is saying, she devotes her entire life to his cause. She is, in fact, the woman we will soon know as Mary Magdalene.

14

THE TEST

Soon after, Jesus performs the second of his 'miraculous' signs. These are explicitly numbered, to encourage us to notice how many there are in total (seven, by the way). This time, the action involves a little boy who is sick, whose father approaches Jesus, to ask that his son be healed. This boy will figure significantly in the sections to follow, so I will move on.

Jesus, as you know, travels constantly between Samaria and Judea. What you may not have realized, is that with every trip into Jerusalem, he gets closer and closer to his adversaries, infiltrating deeper and deeper into their territory. He appeals to the priests within their sacred spaces, he preaches from the inner sanctum, where he should not be allowed, and he makes a mockery of the Temple rules and regulations. Neither is it evident, until much later in the story, that Jesus is also acquiring great throngs of supporters. These aren't the 'weak and the poor' as has been the tradition, but men and women of influence and power. He is gathering known insurgents from across the river, hoards of Samaritans from up North, and a surprising number of converts from within the Temple institution itself. He rapidly proves himself to be a formidable threat to the status quo, and he "isn't alone," as he sometimes likes to make clear.

When the time comes for the famous "feeding of the five thousand," Jesus has reached a watershed moment... and so has Philip, his son. This is Philip's test, to see if he has what it takes to become Jesus' second. Unfortunately, he does not, as he fails to see the symbolic implications of the feeding. In fact, many of Jesus' followers begin to have second thoughts around this time, misinterpreting what he is saying, and failing to grasp the finer points of his campaign.

The thing about the feeding is this: The people are hungry for freedom from oppression. They are seeking a king to deliver them from the Romans. They seek "the Messiah" (in this context, the Davidic, warlike messiah) and will thrust the job upon the first eligible and promising man who comes along, 'root of Jesse' or not! Jesus, however, has no interest in playing the Roman-slayer; he has a more important, long-term mission and tries so very hard to stick to it.

Acting as the Samaritan high priest, Jesus takes control of the Passover meal up on Golan Heights; this is what the feeding scenario is. He takes five loaves and two fish, symbolizing the five sons of Judah and the two sons of Joseph, together representing the united tribes of Israel, e.g., the *twelve* baskets of leftovers. It is so amazingly simple, yet few 'get it'. When Jesus starts talking about eating his "flesh and blood," several take flight, thinking him mad. There is, however, a very rational basis to his allusion, and again, we find it has to do with the reunion of the tribes and the return of the rightful heirs to their "fortunes."

From this point, Jesus knows his mission is going to be more difficult than he had anticipated. Philip disappoints him in his inability to become a leader, but remains a close and special disciple to the end. It has become necessary, however, to seek out a new heir, a new right-hand-man, and quickly.

INSIGHT

Now it is time to get back to the little boy whose father had asked Jesus to cure. This is the character we will soon come to know as Lazarus. Initially, though, he is a boy of twelve, going on thirteen. In Jewish terms, this is considered the rite of passage from childhood to manhood, from innocence to responsibility. It is a time for choosing one's affiliations (e.g., Pharisees, Essenes, Sadducees); it is a symbolic death of one existence, and a rebirth into another.

Indeed, the young boy is near death, but not a physical death. The father, who we deduce to be none other than Nicodemus, seeks Jesus' intervention to break the cycle of ignorance and delusion that generations of his family have experienced, as priests and Pharisees. He asks Jesus, in effect, to take the boy as a protégée, before it is too late. Jesus agrees, but the time is not yet right, so he waits.

When Jesus later comes to the Temple to appeal to the priests, however, he calls out for the special "one" to make himself known. He is sending out the signal that it is now time for the boy to join him. The next time we see the youth, he has earned himself a new commission name – the "blind man."

Once blinded by the world of ignorance and iniquity into which he was born, the young man openly rejects the expectations of his peers and refuses to become both Temple priest and Pharisee. He proudly admits to being Jesus' disciple, and affirms his devotion three times, hinting at a threefold denial that will feature later in the gospel. Jesus, in an unprecedented demonstration of intimacy, anoints the boy's eyes with mud, representing the darkness of the world, the corruption of its ways, its untruths. In washing this mud away, the blind man restores his inner vision; he sees what Jesus wants him to see. The young Lazarus officially becomes Jesus' second, legally his adopted "son."

There is something much more important here, however, than the symbolic spiritual rebirth, though that in itself is vital to the story. What is of paramount significance is the place to which the blind man is sent, when ordered to wash: the Pool of Siloam. *Siloam, basically, is another word for Shiloh.* Not only is the boy's washing at this Pool a confirmation for Jesus that his 'message' is clear and has been acknowledged (the boy accepts his role as Jesus' protégée in the campaign to restore Shiloh as the royal seat), it is fundamental to the entire post-crucifixion scene, for this is the very site where Jesus will be lain to rest on that fateful day. I will come back to this.

The utter audacity, though! Provoking the Pharisees, humiliating them in public is a dangerous business. The authorities take it upon themselves to deal with these troublemakers once and for all, whatever it might take.

BRIDE OF GOD

Meanwhile, Mary's character is becoming more and more important to the plan. She was introduced to us as the Samaritan woman at the well. Remembering the use of commission names, we soon recognize that Mary's role is both symbolic and practical. Symbolically, she plays the most profound character known in the Bible, perhaps, besides that of God... she is the Bride of God. Although this is a complex issue, and deserves much more attention, I do explain it in detail in *Jesus, King of Israel*, but for the purposes of this short *Introduction*, this account will have to suffice:

In Ezekiel 16, the anticipated rescue and restoration of Israel is depicted in terms of a female foundling thrown out to die in the wilderness. Completely helpless, the foundling is inspired (in the literal sense of the word) by the passing "spirit" (breath) of God, and lives. She grows to be a beautiful woman and becomes the beloved of God, his elected one. A covenant is made between the husband (God) and wife (Israel); she is cleansed, anointed and elevated to the highest status. Although married to God, she is seduced from her loyalty to him by the attractions of other (e.g., Canaanite) gods, who are depicted as her illicit lovers. She has become as a "whore" in the eyes of God, and suffers the consequences of his wrath.

> Have you seen what she did, that faithless one, Israel, how she...played the whore...? And I thought, 'After she has done all this she will return to me....' ...I had sent her away with a decree of divorce...
> Jer 3:6-8

19

The bride, in this context the "sister" of Judah, i.e., northern Israel, is charged with adultery and is prepared for trial. It is the act of repentance which determines whether the harlot wife is to be forgiven or stoned. If she is truly ashamed of her behavior, she will be restored to her former glory and reinstated as the beloved companion of God. If she is stubborn, nothing can save her. She is, in the end, forgiven, and the entire process begins again, ending with the ideal of the perfect marriage between Israel and its god.

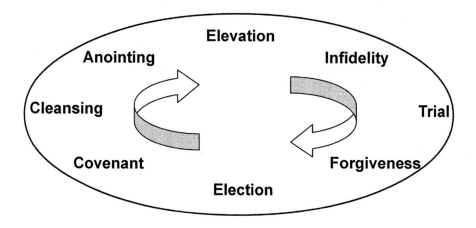

Indeed, we will see Mary rise from the apparent Samaritan harlot, the woman with many husbands and a lover who is not her husband, to a place of unsurpassed honour and glory. It may even be suggested that the legend of Mary being a "prostitute" stemmed from a once recognized, but subsequently misrepresented allusion to this Bride of God theme: in reality, the woman at the well *must* have been a virgin, if she were to be of any consequence to Jesus' plan. Later, in fact, we find that her virginity is actually proved, albeit in a very subtle and indirect biblical reference. For the sake of representing the symbolic rise of the new nation, however, she takes on various roles throughout the gospel.

We have to understand Mary's relationship to the other characters within Jesus' closest circle. She is not, as Dan Brown (and many others) would have us believe, Jesus' wife. Jesus is already married, you see, to Martha, the mistress of the home in Bethany, where Jesus finds safe repose and where Lazarus comes to live. I do not discount the possibility of polygamy, however, as we know it was practiced by some at the time, but given the other details of the case, which I can't go into here, I think it more practical and plausible that Jesus finds an alternative partner for this important woman.

Mary, in effect, is another of Jesus' protégées. She is the symbolic, northern "rod of Joseph" that Jesus will unite with the southern "rod of Judah" (other terms taken from Ezekiel's vision of the restoration of Israel) in preparation for the new, *united* kingdom. Mary, though representing the Bride of God on a symbolic level, *is* also being groomed to be a wife in reality, but not Jesus' wife... Lazarus'.

It is for this reason, I believe, that she is living in Jesus' house, and why she becomes the focus of gossip and insinuation. There are rumors flying that Jesus is behaving badly, that he has moved a mistress into his home, right under his wife's nose. In reality, Martha is acting as chaperone for Mary and Lazarus. Nevertheless, the authorities assume this is a case of adultery, so Mary is seized and brought to trial... the next step in her role as the Bride of God, conveniently enough.

She is brought before the very man who is claiming to be a priest, Jesus that is, in the authorities' bid to expose him as a fraud. Those charged with adultery, you see, were to be judged by a priest, according to law. If Jesus is claiming to be a priest, he must perform his duty. If he does not, he risks weakening his case and losing the support of many of his followers. Again, though, as we know, Jesus beats them at their own game, but he does so in a provocative and chastising manner, accusing the accusers with 'prostituting' *themselves*!

SEVENTH SIGN

As the plot continues in the gospel, Jesus is away when Lazarus apparently falls ill, but we know from our detective work that this illness is a euphemism for Lazarus' being arrested by the Pharisees. They are getting their own back. They seize the young man and incarcerate him in a rock-hewn cell, in the hopes of luring Jesus out of his secure hiding place to the North. If they can get both men with one fell swoop, all the better!

The ruse apparently works, for Jesus does come all the way to Jerusalem to rescue his adopted "son," his heir, Lazarus, but he does it in such a clever way that the authorities can do nothing but watch them both walk away, much to their chagrin.

Not only has Jesus arrived with helpers who do his 'dirty work' for him, by breaking Lazarus free, he has succeeded in turning this otherwise precarious situation into a victory for his cause. Lazarus' enforced confinement serves as his initiation, his rite of passage into Jesus' new priesthood. The symbolism is intentional and not just for the benefit of the gospel readers – it was probably perfectly evident to the Pharisees at the time. We learn, for instance, that "Lazarus," as a commission name, holds several intriguing surprises, not least of which is the fact that it relates to the *'azara*, the Court of Israel and the Court of the Priests. By having Lazarus raised up on the third day (recall that Jesus delays for two days), Jesus can snub the authorities who once scoffed at his claim to raise the Temple again in three days.

In fact, this further humiliation seals both Lazarus' and Jesus' fate, as far as the Pharisees and the priests are concerned, and death warrants are issued.

With respect to the gospel's numbered signs, though, this proves to be the culminating seventh sign of Jesus' entire mission, anticipated and hinted at throughout the gospel. It is the moment of glory Jesus has been waiting for, the moment of emancipation his plan needed. It is the moment of glory for Lazarus and the turning point for his relationship with Mary.

NAZARITE

Mary's anointing scene marks another turning point. Once again, we find that tradition has placed its foot heavily on the neck of truth, for Mary is far from a 'woman of ill repute' using her oils to seduce Jesus. If you follow the clues in the gospel, you discover that she is actually going through her *own* anointing, here, as she has sworn her devotion to the cause and is now becoming a nazarite (and yes, I use a small "n," as in the original Greek). Being a nazarite meant you were swearing your allegiance to something or someone. In Samuel's case, it was to God, in Paul's case, to (his perception of) Jesus. The nazarite was to have his/her head, i.e., hair, anointed and was forbidden to cut it for the prescribed duration of the sacred vow. Mary's one recognizable feature is her long hair. This is the first sign of her symbolic rise; she has been outcast, ridiculed, set on trial, and forgiven – now she begins her ascent to become the Bride.

We also find that the oil she is using is not some potion from the prostitute's toolbox, but is, in fact, a new blend of the holy anointing oil, intended only for the Temple and its priest. By claiming to have the anointing oil, you see, Jesus is once again proving his superiority over the Temple cultus, who have not been anointed for generations. It is for this reason Judas takes offence.

A Note on Judas:

Though there is no room for an extensive account of Judas, or other of the disciples, here, it is helpful for you to know that in *Jesus, King of Israel*, I claim that Judas is the character later referred to as

Barabbas (a commission name). He is a chief priest of the Temple, sent to infiltrate Jesus' inner circle, and duty bound to report his findings to the high priest.

HOLY FAMILY OF EPHRAIM

Let's just recap for a moment.

Jesus, a Samaritan seeking the restoration of his people's inheritance, i.e., the seat at the right hand of God, the royal throne as once promised to Joseph, has returned from an insightful life abroad, to draw the remnant of like-believers back into one, strong fold. He has his eye on the throne of a united Israel, and sets a plan in motion to oust the authority that is centered in Judea and assert a new priestly kingdom at Shiloh. He amasses support, especially in the North, and he has found a trustworthy right-hand-man, the young Lazarus.

He knows, however, that time is running out. One cannot ridicule and offend the Pharisees for long, without retribution. In order to have a priestly kingdom, as specified by God at Sinai, one must create a dynasty. The roles of high priest and king are intertwined, mutually supportive – and they are also hereditary. Jesus *needs* an heir.

Yes, he has Lazarus, but he is an adopted heir, appointed because circumstances dictated, but he is not a blood relative. What happens to the kingdom if there is no direct descent from the first high priest, no 'divinely ordained' lineage? Jesus wants to ensure this is set in motion before it is too late. His wife, Martha, is aging (as is Jesus himself) and we see that she is not quite on the same wavelength as Jesus, as far as his mission is concerned. She is dutiful and although she does as she is told, I can readily perceive her to be adverse to

27

bearing another child just to fit into Jesus' rather dangerous and off-the-wall plan. Though, probably, the times would have dictated that she conceive, regardless, she might be too old to have more children, or Jesus simply doesn't think the conception will be fortuitous, given Martha's reticence.

There is also a more significant, symbolic necessity for finding another mother figure, however: the reunion of the tribes. Jesus has to find a way of fulfilling the prophecy that speaks of combining the "rods of Judah and Israel," before the Messiah can come and the nation can be restored. That is, he must create a union between someone from the North and someone from the South. Mary is a Samaritan, like Jesus and Martha. Either Jesus needs to marry a southerner, or Mary needs to.

Lazarus, we discover, is from the tribe of Benjamin, a southerner. Mary and Lazarus are thus groomed for their eventual marriage, and even the patterns of incidents and literary structure in the gospel affirm their parallel raison d'être. As always, however, and this is why you really need your wits about you when you delve into the gospel looking for clues, there is an ambiguity surrounding the marriage (which itself is not made *explicit*) that makes you wonder who is really the "bridegroom": *is* it Lazarus... or Jesus?

But that's the whole point, really. The entire gospel is written in such a way that either Jesus or Lazarus can be seen as the central figure. Their roles are inextricably linked and intertwining, just like those of the (true) high priest and king. This is very intentional, on the part of the gospel author, as we will see.

So, Jesus sets up a marriage between Mary and Lazarus. The only thing is, somewhere 'between the lines' of the story, Mary has become pregnant. Who is the father? Again, there is no concrete evidence for attributing the pregnancy to Jesus, yet neither is their for saying it must be Lazarus. Several clues, though, lead us to a satisfactory conclusion that Jesus is probably the father, but Lazarus takes on the responsibility of parenthood.

Recall the story of Mary and Joseph that stems from the Synoptic gospels and other apocryphal texts. Mary, a young woman, is mysteriously found pregnant. She is betrothed to a man called Joseph who, according to most versions, knows he is not the father of her child, but agrees to marry her anyway, taking on the responsibility of the 'sacred' son. This unit becomes known as the "Holy Family." Well, what I claim is that the Holy Family of Mary, Joseph, and Child, refers not to Jesus and his parents, but to Mary Magdalene, Lazarus (who will later take on the commission name of Joseph of Arimathea), and the new heir to the priestly kingdom at Shiloh. Everything fits.

Now, when Mary becomes a nazarite, I think she has already given birth to her son – symbolically, in Ephraim. Naturally, there are clues that lead me to this conclusion. It is after the boy has been circumcised that Jesus feels secure in returning to Jerusalem, for all to see... and this is where things really start to get interesting.

Most scholars suggest Jesus enters Jerusalem on that historic day, through the Eastern Gate. This is based, whether Christians are aware or not, on the interpretation of various biblical references to "the Messiah" coming through the Eastern Gate. We know now that Jesus rejects the common notion of the messiah-king, and is adhering to the role of the Samaritan priestly messiah. Why would he pander to those he rejects, by claiming to be the one thing he adamantly opposes? (The question of Jesus' own perception regarding the advent of "the Messiah" is complicated, but it has to do, primarily, with understanding that the role is divinely, not humanly, attributed, and not dependent on the family line of David.) No, I think Jesus returns to Jerusalem in triumph because he has succeeded in doing what he claimed he would do: he has 'rebuilt' the new 'Temple' and ensured both a hereditary and anointed line – something the current institution cannot match.

He rides in, I argue, through the *northern* Gate of Ephraim. The new family has just come from that town, making the trajectory and symbolic significance much more in keeping, but what makes the clues here so fascinating is the fact that the Gate of Ephraim is also known as the Fish Gate. What was the first symbol for Jesus to be used amongst his followers? The fish. Thus, the symbol of the fish originally implied recognition of Jesus' northern roots and his claim to the Samaritan-based Israelite throne!

We learn, also, later in the gospel, that in her role as mother of the new dynastic heir, Mary is depicted as a "Gate Keeper," making subtle reference to the Gate of Ephraim, the Child of Ephraim, whom she protects.

RIVALRY

Two thousand years of being told that Peter was Jesus' chosen successor is hard to refute, but the Gospel of John never once places Peter in such a role. If anything, this gospel makes it very clear that it is Lazarus whom Jesus entrusts with this responsibility. Lazarus becomes Jesus' heir elect, the regent who will rule after Jesus, until the child is "of age." He becomes Jesus' deputy high priest and, in keeping with the ambiguity mentioned before, he takes on the roles and duties of his adoptive father to such an extent, it is hard to distinguish between the two characters. This is made most evident during the burial scenario (later).

Lazarus, the young lad who has proven himself time and again, versus the old man, Peter... this is a rivalry in the making, and the gospel does make the most of it in portraying the schism between Jesus' path and the path that would lead others to Christianity.

Peter first enters the scene early in the gospel, as the lame man by the Sheep Gate. In *Jesus, King of Israel*, I reveal how Peter represents the weakened and rather pathetic common priesthood, who are all but dominated by the politics and ambitions of the chief-priestly clans. In the scene where Jesus apparently orders the lame man to walk, he is, in essence, telling Peter and his fellow priests that they have it within themselves to reject this unsanctioned authority and take matters into their own hands. Many do, in fact, and we soon learn that Jesus is converting numerous 'ordinary priests' to his cause. Peter, however, begins his characterization with dubious sincerity, and is the first to point the finger when the Pharisees come looking for Jesus. We don't hear anything else about him, until now.

Now that Jesus is looking like he might just be successful, we suddenly find Peter being somewhat obsequious, grovelling, trying to show himself worthy of more attention. Remember the idea I mentioned earlier, about the 'rights of the firstborn' and the rightful heir? Well, Peter seems to see himself as the 'firstborn' of Jesus' new group. He anticipates inheriting the rights and privileges of that rank, but when he learns of Lazarus' significance to Jesus, he gets jealous. The tension builds throughout the gospel, with Peter constantly trying to show that he is better than Lazarus. In the foot-washing scene, for instance, Peter insists on twice the cleansing (the washing of both feet *and* hands), which is synonymous with the share of the firstborn (twice the lot of the others). Repeatedly, Peter is tested, given opportunities to show his trustworthiness and faith, but in every instance he succumbs to his own ambition and defiance.

This nature is aptly represented in his nickname, "Cephas." We learn that Cephas, far from meaning "rock" (as in bedrock, i.e., the foundation of the Church), actually means "hollowed out rock" or "to bend down"; it implies some sort of weakness. Following the clues, we soon discover that Peter is, from the very start of the gospel, someone who is a liability and who needs to be disciplined, if he is to "follow" Jesus. Ultimately, he fails to prove himself.

Of course, the biggest *faux pas* Peter has to overcome in the eyes of all subsequent Christians, is the fact that he betrays Jesus, just when he is most needed and most able to demonstrate his otherwise loudly attested support. What I investigate in my book, however, is the degree to which Peter uses his allegiance with Judas to safeguard his own interests. It's as if he still hasn't quite made up his mind where he stands, so he hedges his bets. He sides with Judas, just in case Jesus fails miserably and all is doomed on that front; he can then go quietly back to his comfortable job, with little retribution. On the other hand, he doesn't openly defy Jesus, just in case there is a chance he will still win a larger portion of the ultimate prize.

By the end of the story, in the gospel's Epilogue (John 21), which I claim was written at the time of Lazarus' death, Peter is clearly subordinated to the rest of the disciples, who have themselves been fully initiated as "ministers" of the new order. I think this section of the gospel was written for the sole purpose of reestablishing the order of authority in the new group Jesus had formed. It seems Peter wanted his own authority so much, he set up his own clique of like-minded, probably aging, priests, in opposition to the 'pip-squeak' Lazarus' band of twelve. It was thus Peter's more mainstream following that eventually gave birth to the Christian tradition.

ARREST

By the time Jesus is arrested, not in the Garden of Gethsemene, but in the King's Garden, Lazarus has acquired another commission name, i.e., Malthus. This is his role as Jesus' deputy: a deputy high priest was appointed if the high priest was incapacitated, in some way, and could not perform his duties on the Day of Atonement. Again, by following very specific clues regarding the use of time, calendrical references, and scriptural allusions, we learn that Jesus' day of execution is actually his own, symbolic Day of Atonement. We also see how Peter, armed and ready for trouble, attempts to disqualify Lazarus (Malthus) for the post, by cutting off his ear (a maimed priest normally could not serve).

In my book, I argue that the route Jesus was forced to take that night, to Annas' office, included an occult passage under the Temple – a passage Josephus writes about. The entire procession, from Jesus' entry into that passage, to his reemergence en route to Caiaphas' house, includes Temple areas named after "hearth" and "flame" (referring to the fire around which the guards warm themselves); "vestments" (referring to Jesus' priestly vestments, all of which are mentioned in the gospel, and which become one of the main focuses of the crucifixion scene); "slaughterhouse" and "altar" (referring to Jesus being a sacrifice); and even "scapegoat" (Jesus becomes the scapegoat for Caiaphas). It is a wonderfully coherent and deeply symbolic allusion to Jesus' entire mission, ironically put in action by the very people seeking his demise.

What few scholars or theologians have managed to account for, satisfactorily, however, is why Jesus was arrested at all. So he bent the rules and challenged the status quo; but if all he does is help sick people and try to promote loving one's enemies, what is so desperately annoying or potentially dangerous that the authorities want him dead? The only way this all makes sense is if Jesus is truly seen as a threat to Judean primacy. He is a political, indeed a royal pretender. He is clever, sophisticated, has friends in high places, and is charismatic. He has the potential to rally three quarters of Israel (the nine 'lost' tribes, versus the three in Judea) to his cause. This is no ordinary Messiah wannabe.

The reason for Jesus' arrest is simple, and it is recorded in history, if we only had a clear enough vision to see it earlier. Josephus tells of a Samaritan leader who takes a throng of followers up Mount Gerizim to reveal to them the site of the Ark of the Covenant. Seeing this outlandish display as a revolt against Rome (so he would claim later), Pilate responds by having the crowd all but slaughtered. The leader escapes, but is under a sentence of death.

Now, there are ways and means of discerning how Jesus fits this character, but the point is, Josephus is writing about a Samaritan upstart who claims unique knowledge and who is ultimately condemned to death by the procurator. Interestingly, the Messiah ben Joseph tradition I discussed earlier has a bearing on this, as he was said to be responsible for the 'downfall' (or death) of the procurator. Pilate was, indeed, withdrawn from Palestine and sent back to Rome, castigated over this messy incident.

There are also reflections of 2 Esdras, where the "man who came down from the mountain" is described in terms of being in a great crowd that is attacked, and of possessing the Ark of the Covenant.

While the issue of the Ark is a thread that runs through the other book (*Jesus, King of Israel*), there is little room for it do be discussed here. Needless to say, however, Jesus does seem to at least claim that he knows where the Ark is. Without it, it would seem, his own assertion to divinely-ordained rights (with respect to his new priestly kingdom), would mean little.

JUDAS BARABBAS

The story of Barabbas and Jesus before Pilate, and the crowds making the final decision about who will die and who will be set free is pure Hollywood. I mean, it makes for great drama and spectacle. In actual fact, the truth of the matter, as told in the gospel, makes even *better* movie fodder!

Barabbas, who, as I said earlier, is Judas, represents the Temple priesthood. He is only there because Pilate is fed up with the chief priests attempting to manipulate and coerce him into satisfying their own needs. He is not a man to be toyed with. When Jesus is finally captured, Judas is taken, too, as a snub to the institution that dared to provoke the representative of Rome. There is no competition, in reality, for the chief priests want their own man back and they have influence over the crowd.

I don't think there was a choice, in *fact*. I believe the famous "Paschal Pardon" referred to the ritualistic handing-over of the priestly vestments at Passover, which were otherwise kept under lock and key by the Romans. The allusion is more than apt, however, when you think of the gospel writer trying to convey a powerful image of the people "choosing" Jesus' new path or rejecting it. In effect, they "choose" the status quo; they elect Barabbas, i.e., the current Temple cultus, despite its iniquities and weaknesses – that is the point being made here.

Though the story of Judas' (Barabbas') demise is not, strictly speaking, mentioned in the Gospel of John, there are plenty of extraneous clues to suggest that he, too, is crucified (as opposed to committing suicide)… right next to Jesus, in fact.

ESCAPE

As Jesus hangs on the cross, Martha, Lazarus, and Mary stand near. Jesus hands his wife over to the charge of his adopted son, Lazarus, who is in his penultimate guise as Joseph of Arimathea. Elsewhere, I explain how each commission name works, but Lazarus' are so very important; they form the entire key to understanding the gospel, and hence, understanding the story of Jesus, Mary, and the kingdom at Shiloh.

By now, Mary, too, has continued in her rise to becoming the Bride of God, and her commission names change to reflect that honour. Everything seems to be fitting into place for the final push to Shiloh. But wait… isn't Jesus about to be killed?

Well, no. There has been a plan in the works since Jesus' escape from Mount Gerizim, if not before, that when he is captured, and most probably crucified (which is the standard form of capital punishment by the Romans, and Jesus *knows* Pilate is after him), Lazarus and Nicodemus will rescue him. He will then make his way up to Shiloh, in order to be there on the sacred "third day," to inaugurate the new kingdom, as the prophecies foretell.

The plan is for Lazarus and Nicodemus to administer a strong sedative, so Jesus will appear to die quickly, thus sparing him the breaking of the legs, a tactic used to hasten death. He is given the potion on a branch of hyssop, which we find plays a significant role in the ritual cleansing of those who have come into contact with the dead. The symbolism allows us to see that Jesus goes through a prescribed period of ritual cleansing after his close encounter with death, one that includes avoiding being touched by any other person not ritually cleansed (hence the subsequent order for Mary not to touch him).

Jesus' body is then requested, and the two men get to work feigning a hasty burial. They wrap Jesus up in broad sheets of linen, rather than the usual bands, in an effort to conceal the supplies of anointing oil which they must take with them to Shiloh. (When you analyze the crucifixion scene, you find clues to the weights and ingredients of the oils brought to the site. It turns out the oils brought to Jesus' "tomb" correspond exactly with those of the original holy anointing oil.) These loose sheets also enable Jesus to free himself when he regains consciousness, should the others not be there to help him.

Where is Jesus' burial site? This is important, and everything in the gospel thus far has been hinting at it! Where did Jesus send the young blind man to be initiated into the 'secret' of Shiloh? The Pool of Siloam! The site of Golgotha, which I claim to be the Mount of Destruction on the southeast corner of Jerusalem, is opposite the King's Garden and the Pool of Siloam, making it the perfect place (for several other reasons, too) for Jesus' site of crucifixion. If his burial is, indeed, as hasty as we are led to believe, and as temporary, it has to be convenient. The tunnel at the Pool of Siloam is ideal.

It is also the focus of a strong series of allusions to historical/ biblical precedents for *escapes*. We even learn the actual timing and the route of Jesus' escape from the simple reference to this tunnel.

It is while in this makeshift tomb that we witness the true "raising of Lazarus," for he undergoes his own anointing, becoming not just

40

deputy, but fully-fledged high priest. The ambiguity I alerted you to, regarding the characters of Jesus and Lazarus, and especially as they relate to Mary, is highlighted here, when Mary stumbles upon the "two angels" in the darkness of the tunnel. Presuming one to be Jesus, she is stunned to find her husband Lazarus (now Joseph, remember) in the place where Jesus should be. She calls him by the same name of respect as she does Jesus, and her actions convince us that Jesus and Lazarus are now indistinguishable, as far as their roles are concerned.

The tunnel at the Pool of Siloam also reminds us of another prophecy regarding the birth of a child who will mark the advent of a new age, and of a reference to the anointing of the King of Israel… pretty powerful allusions (but you really need to read about them in context, along with the other clues).

SUCCESSOR

On the "third day," Christian tradition holds, Jesus was resurrected, for the disciples found his "tomb" empty... right? In fact, what happens in the Gospel of John is something rather more pragmatic.

When Mary first arrives at the entrance to the tunnel, to find the two "angels" standing where Jesus once lay, it is not the third day, but the second... the very morning after the crucifixion. The two men in white are actually Nicodemus and Lazarus, symbolically situated at both the feet (Nicodemus) and the head (Lazarus) of their master's once reclining body. The only things left in Jesus' place are his burial garments and a rolled up turban which, we discover, is one of the sacred vestments of the high priest. The rolling up and handing over of the turban signifies the transference of office. Lazarus is becoming the new high priest at this moment – besides, Peter is rushing to the scene, and he must be convinced, once and for all, that it is Lazarus whom Jesus has chosen as successor. By seeing Lazarus with this token of office, the message should be very clear.

With the process of tending Jesus' wounds, reviving him enough to be able to travel, and disguising him as the "gardener" to avoid recognition, Lazarus, Nicodemus, and Mary (presumably with the child and Martha in tow) set out for the most important trek of their lives, from the hiding place of the "conduit" south east of Jerusalem, to the long-anticipated site of the new throne of Israel, Shiloh. By the third day, according to prophecy, they make it.

The other disciples, barring Peter, have made their way there in advance and are awaiting Jesus in a secret location, closed to outsiders. They have each undergone a seven-day initiation confined in a locked space, just as Lazarus had endured. They are all priests, now, except for Peter. He is noticeably absent when the others receive the "Holy Spirit."

We find this confused and somewhat pathetic disciple up to his old tricks again, siding with the one person he thinks more powerful, or successful. When Judas is executed, Peter realizes it is safer for him to disappear from Jerusalem. We soon find him joining the group of disciples up in Shiloh, but this time, under the commission name of "Thomas." That's right, the famous "Doubting Thomas" is none other than Peter, the fickle, unreliable old priest who can never quite make the grade, as far as Jesus is concerned.

When Peter hears from the others that Jesus is there, that he is alive and the plan for Shiloh is going ahead, he cannot believe it. Jesus appears, wounds still fresh, but the ritual cleansing after his exposure to the dead complete. Although he offers Peter the opportunity to "touch" and therefore "believe," there is much more to this scene than meets the eye, as this is the moment of truth for Peter.

In order to reach down and touch Jesus' side, Peter must lower his head. Will he "bend down," as his nickname "Cephas" implies, will he humble himself by lowering his head before Jesus? We are not told that he does. Similarly, in the gospel's Epilogue (Chapter 21), when Jesus tells Peter to follow, we are left in suspense, never really knowing if he does or not, until later books in the New Testament carry on where that story leaves off, and we find Peter hasn't followed Jesus, but is leading his own little army of priests.

LIKE FATHER LIKE SON

So, we know that Jesus and Lazarus make it to Shiloh. They inaugurate the new priesthood there. They establish the priestly-royal dynasty, with Mary Magdalene as the mother of Jesus' son, and Lazarus, the dutiful, loyal husband who serves as regent until the boy becomes old enough to represent Israel. But what happens then?

There are a few references in other New Testament texts that further reveal Peter's rivalry with Lazarus. There are some letters from Paul that indicate he is forcefully trying to downplay, if not eradicate, the Gospel of John: its promulgators are deemed heretics, its message heresy. What message could possibly be heretical? That the rightful heir, the firstborn, *has* been resurrected – restored to the right hand of God. That means the northern tribes are once again united and powerful – a daunting prospect for the Judeans *and* the Romans! Of course, this is primarily a conceptual victory, at this point, but Jesus has certainly amassed enough support for any further demonstration of his success to be like a spark in a tinderbox. Paul is sent, according to some authorities, to control this new, dangerous situation. He does so as a skilled diplomat, changing the story of Jesus, the man, forever.

There is also a very discreet reference to a young boy, called "Mark," in one of the letters attributed to Peter (but which I argue is probably the work of the same person who wrote the Gospel of John). This child, Mark, has a mother who was "chosen" at the same time as the disciples. Mother and child are said to be "in Babylon," which is a synonym for the gentile world, suggesting they have been taken away to relative safety (hence the legend of Joseph of Arimathea taking a certain Mary abroad, for her own protection. This Mary is the Magdalene, however, *not* Jesus' mother – and Joseph of Arimathea, recall, is Lazarus!). The *author* of this particular letter suggests he shares in Jesus' glory. Indeed, as high priest and regent, *Lazarus* does share Jesus' glory!

To learn more about Jesus and the Holy Family beyond this, we must deviate from the Gospel of John and other biblical texts and head into more historical documents, especially the writings of Josephus. As I said before, there are two major references to Jesus in Josephus, and all but the most diehard Christian critics now agree these are later insertions. These were suitably placed in the most important work relating to the history of the Jews by Christians who failed to find any reference to their now familiar figure of "Christ." The thing is, with just a little slant on the perspective, one can find *several* original references to the characters that have become visible in the Gospel of John, most especially Jesus the Samaritan, Mary and Lazarus, and their son. They are all there.

There is, for instance, a diatribe against Mary, the mother of a child who is sacrificed in an uncannily symbolic way, i.e., to preserve life. In order to preserve life, Mary, we are told, *eats* her child. The "flesh and the blood" speech, it seems, was never lived down, and even by the time of Josephus, this one 'sensational' aspect of the early Jesus Movement seems to have grown into an urban legend!

There are many potential clues in Josephus, and I try to mention

46

most of the immediately relevant ones in *Jesus, King of Israel*, but the one that is of most significance here, is, perhaps, the reference to Jesus, son of Ananus. The tale of this remarkable character includes several parallels to that of our Jesus: he demonstrates at the Temple during festivals, is arrested by the Jews, then presented to the procurator. He is interrogated and flogged, says little, and is deemed mad. Rather than being crucified, however, he is released, only to resurface during the fall of the Temple, where he is last heard bemoaning the fate of Israel. He dies uttering his lamentations.

When we analyze the subtleties a little closer, however, we realize that this Jesus, son of Ananus, is most likely the mysterious child of the gospel and "Mark" in the aforementioned letter. He, too, travels abroad, but returns to 'finish the works of his father'. He takes his father's name, begins his ministry at about the same age, and dies defending his father's ideals, but probably not before making sure *he* has an heir, too… the identity and whereabouts of *this* "son of Joseph" is the greatest mystery of all!

As for Jesus, and the kingdom at Shiloh, I suggest he lives out his days there, and is buried by his "beloved disciple," Lazarus, on a particular hill overlooking the sacred site. I believe there is, indeed, a grave to be found for Jesus – it's just not where people have presumed it to be.

Mary, the child, and Lazarus flee to safety – who knows how long after the inauguration at Shiloh. But the new kingdom has been created, and the gospel written as a road map for the remnant of believers – a map for both soul and body. Jesus rests in his homeland, keeping a solemn vigil over the Ark of the Covenant, and the dynasty probably lives on, somewhere, awaiting the perfect moment for its revelation to the world.

Jesus, King of Israel
Samaritan Blood and the Kingdom at Shiloh

Discover the full story… follow all of the clues! If you have been intrigued by this summary of the book about Jesus, Mary, Lazarus, and Child, and want to learn more, you will find in *Jesus, King of Israel*:

- the meaning behind each name in the gospel

- an explanation for the use of numbers, times, and dates

- an account of Jesus' relationship with John the Baptist

- the significance of the Essenes

- the symbolic use of weights and measures

- a full description of the 2 Esdras parallels, especially the Uriel-Ezra dialogue

- the explanation for a revised location of Golgotha

- the meaning behind the "mercy seat" and Gabbatha

- a description of the mysterious place called Arzareth

- the identity of the *"parakletos"*

- further details concerning the raising of Lazarus

- full accounts of the post-crucifixion scenes

- a detailed explanation for each of the seven signs

…and much, much more!

JESUS
KING OF ISRAEL

Samaritan Blood and the
Kingdom at Shiloh

J. S. Tyson

ISBN 0-9735341-5-X
336pp (290pp + Appendix, Bibliography & Index)
6 x 9 Paperback
$22.95 (US) $30.95 (CAD)

If you have enjoyed this book, and would like to share its contents with someone else, why not send them a gift of it? We will gladly send a person of your choice a FREE copy of *Before the Da Vinci Code*, together with a note saying it is a gift from you (if you wish).

Just fill in the form below (may be photocopied), or email us at **sales@eccenova.com** (shipping & handling fees can be posted or paid through **www.paypal.com**, using the same email address). Send to: **EcceNova (Sales), 308-640 Dallas Road, Victoria, BC, V8V 1B6, Canada**

Please send a **FREE COPY** of this book, *Before the Da Vinci Code*, to the following person:

Name:

Address:

Postal Code:

Country:

I enclose a shipping/handling fee of US$5

Please enclose a note saying the book is a gift from:

Printed in the United States
31845LVS00001B/207

9 780973 534177